REFLECTIONS

ON

THE OPERATION

OF THE

PRESENT SYSTEM OF EDUCATION.

BY

CHRISTOPHER C. ANDREWS,

COUNSELLOR AT LAW.

"TRAIN UP A CHILD IN THE WAY HE SHOULD GO; AND, WHEN HE IS OLD, HE WILL NOT DEPART FROM IT."

BOSTON:

CROSBY, NICHOLS, AND COMPANY,

111, WASHINGTON STREET.

1853.

BOSTON:

PRINTED BY JOHN WILSON AND SON,

22, SCHOOL STREET.

PREFATORY NOTE.

THE increasing importance of the subject treated of has led the author to revise an article, published nearly two years ago in a monthly journal, and to present it in the following pages. His object is to call attention to what he regards a *defect in the operation* of our present system of education, and to propose some suggestions for its remedy. That defect consists in the want of moral instruction in our schools. Its existence, he believes, may be attributed to the state of public opinion, rather than to any imperfection in the system itself. For this reason, he is of opinion that remarks on the subject are more necessary, and therefore worthier of the consideration and indulgence of the public.

35, COURT STREET, BOSTON,
May, 1853.

THE

INCOMPLETE OPERATION

OF OUR

PRESENT SYSTEM OF EDUCATION.

The duty of bringing up the young in the way of usefulness has ever been acknowledged as of utmost importance to the well-being and safety of a State. So imperative was this obligation considered by Solon, the Athenian lawgiver, that he excused children from maintaining their parents, when old and feeble, if they had neglected to qualify them for some useful art or profession. Although this principle has universally prevailed in every civilized age, yet the success of its practical operation depends entirely upon what is understood by necessary knowledge and useful employment. If, as among the Lacedemonians and many other nations of antiquity, a useful art consisted chiefly in the exploits of war, — in being able to undergo privations and hardships, and in wielding successfully the heavy instruments of bloodshed,— such an education as would conduce to the acquirement of that art must be estimated on different grounds from that system whose object is to develop the moral and intellectual faculties.

From the distant past, traditions have come down, evincing in many instances exemplary care in the culture of youth; but the conspicuous record made of them by the historian and poet refutes the idea that they were common. With the lapse of centuries, revolutions in the arts and sciences have been effected, important in themselves, but more so for the changes they have produced both in social and political affairs. Like hunters who discover in their forest-wanderings a valuable mine which shapes anew their course of life, the people of the old world, in the fourteenth and fifteenth centuries, were allured from their incessant conflicts by the more profitable arts of peace. Till then the interests of learning had been crushed by the superstition and bigotry of the times. In the fourteenth century even, the most celebrated university in Europe, that of Bologna, bestowed its chief honors upon the professorship of astrology. But these grand developments in art and science gave a new impulse to social life. Thenceforward the interests of education began to thrive. The patronage given to popular instruction by many of the rulers of European States has imparted a lustre to their annals, which will almost atone for their heartless perversion of human rights. For whether we consider the coercive system of Prussia, which not yet exhibits very happy practical results; or the Austrian system, which indirectly operates coercively by denying employment to those unprovided with school-diplomas; or the Bavarian, which makes a certificate of six years' schooling necessary to the contracting of a valid marriage or apprenticeship; or, indeed, the systems of many other Continental countries, — we find much to excite cheering anticipations.

This country — this Commonwealth especially — has ever been distinguished for being foremost in the maintenance of a benevolent and comprehensive system of education. That system is, we believe, in the judgment of foreigners, one of the most original things which America has produced. Fortunately for the prosperity of the people who derive their support on this rugged soil, their fathers were a class of men deeply imbued with moral sentiment, — lovers of freedom and of knowledge; men who sought that security of their principles in the spread of moral intelligence, which the sword alone would in vain attempt to procure. "The hands that wielded the axe or guided the canoe in the morning opened the page of history and philosophy in the evening;" and it cannot be a matter of surprise, that, counting their greatest wealth in their own industry and resolution, they should at an early period turn their attention to the important subject of education; and that they even denied themselves many of the comforts of life, in order to secure the blessings which might evolve therefrom.

The peculiarity of our system of government is, that it invests the sovereignty in the people; and, as it has always been the policy of every nation claiming to be civilized to educate those who were designed to govern, it might naturally enough be inferred, that, in this country, means would be provided whereby the whole people might receive an education. And thus it is. The true object, therefore, of such a system of instruction as the government supports, it must be conceded by all, consists in qualifying the young to become good citizens, — in teaching them not only what their duties are, but making them ready and willing to perform them. We should discriminate between the object of common schools and the object of colleges; between an institution intended to inform every one of what every one should know, and one designed to fit persons for particular spheres of life, by a course of instruction which it is impracticable for all to pursue. A very large majority of those who enter our colleges are desirous of acquiring that knowledge, as well as discipline, which will prepare them most thoroughly for some one of the learned professions: it is a course preparatory to one still higher, — a gateway by which the industrious and sagacious may with greater ease traverse the long and winding avenues of science. Of a more general nature is the object of that instruction provided by the State for all, because it is designed to fit them for a greater variety of duties, and the chief of these duties is that of *living justly.* If we regarded physical resources as the chief elements of prosperity, or intellectual superiority the principal source of national greatness; if we followed the theory of the Persian legislator, Zoroaster, who thought that to plant a tree, to cultivate a field, and to have a family, were the great duties of man, we might be content with that instruction which would sharpen the intellect, and furnish us with acute and skilful men of business. But an enlightened public sentiment rejects such a theory as narrow and unsafe. It is surely of great importance that children should be made familiar with the common branches of knowledge; that their minds should receive as thorough discipline as is practicable; but

2

of what transcendent importance is it that they should have impressed upon their minds the principles of truth and justice, and the true value of resolute, earnest industry; that they should grow up in the love of virtue and honor, and be taught to know and govern themselves! Education of the heart, as well as education of the mind, should be promoted. The State should make men before it makes artisans; citizens before it makes statesmen. And this in theory it proposes to do. The highest praise that can be bestowed upon our system of education, here in Massachusetts, is that the leading object it contemplates is the moral instruction of the young. This is its grand and peculiar feature. Those who have been and are now at the head of our educational interests, have sought, by timely word and deed, to carry this purpose into active operation. In so doing, they have attempted to give effect to the law which expressly ordains that "all instructors of youth shall exert their best endeavors to impress on the minds of children and youth committed to their care and instruction, the principles of piety, justice, and a sacred regard to truth, love to their country, humanity and universal benevolence, sobriety, industry and frugality, chastity, moderation and temperance, and those other virtues which are the ornament of human society, and the basis upon which a republican constitution is founded; and it shall be the duty of such instructors to endeavor to lead their pupils, as their ages and capacities will admit, into a clear understanding of the tendency of the above-mentioned virtues." (Rev. Stat. chap. 23, § 7.)

Nobody, probably, at this day believes, that, in cherishing principles of this nature, the law which creates this system is visionary or impracticable. All are ready to admit, that the human heart needs the influence of moral discipline. Yet such is the nature of our social existence that there is a great tendency to postpone its application, — to let it depend upon contingencies. When nearly all of the good or evil that we can possibly do has been done, — after temptations have been resisted or yielded to, — after our years begin to wane, we then think seriously of moral improvement. Preachers the most eloquent — for their eloquence commands the highest reward — we employ to exhort us to practise virtues, which, if we had been rightly educated, we should have practised from our earliest youth with as much facility as we read or write. If a child is to learn grammar, let him commence, every one will say, when young, while his memory is most retentive. If we are to teach him those principles which are to shape his destiny in life, and have their home in the heart, should we wait till it is least susceptible of impression? It cannot be denied that too much indifference prevails on this subject. We are apt to shut our eyes to the evils which arise from imperfect education, so long as they do not affect our personal interest. Victims of depraved appetites and passions we take charge of, not out of regard for them, or the circumstances which have induced their guilt, but for our own protection. When a man sunk in crime is held up to public gaze, nearly the same feeling is excited which actuates boys who follow with noisy jests a drunken woman. Rarely do we stop to inquire, why, if wrong influences had been brought to bear upon our characters, we should not have been as bad. Unless such instruction be promoted, many who are now unconcerned for the misfortunes of others will themselves ask for compassion. "Surely there will come a time," says Dr. Johnson with truthful energy, "when he who laughs at wickedness in his companion *shall start from it in his child.*"

Now, the only sure and legitimate way of reforming those evils which burden society is to prevent their acquiring any existence. It is a favorite notion with many, that, by checking vice here and there, our benevolent institutions are working a thorough cure. But this is not so. While we furnish subsistence to those whom intemperance and idleness have brought to destitution, — while we erect asylums where reason may be restored to the shattered mind, — while we enlarge prisons in which to punish the violators of the law, — we should remember that some endeavors should be made to prevent others from requiring the same charities, and incurring the same penalties. Instead of standing merely by the fatal shoal to rescue the sinking crew, we should raise a warning signal to avert future shipwrecks.

All experience shows that, to operate successfully, this branch of education must be early attended to. True it is, that, just as 'the twig is bent, the tree's inclined;' and true it is, that on the discipline of childhood depends the moral character of manhood. The tree in the forest, after it has grown to a considerable height, may yet be bent from its natural course, and, by long-continued force, be made to grow in a different direction; but that change will not be permanent. When the power which turned its course is withdrawn, every breeze and every tempest that shake its branches will aid it in gradually assuming its original position, till hardly a trace of that power which attempted to guide its growth can be perceived. There may be some who would neglect that moral influence on the young which is necessary, trusting in the delusive expectation, that the law will keep them in the right path; that the example of punishment, the terror of the gallows, the prison, or the penitentiary, will prevent the commission of crime. But let us not wait for the saving influence of these things; for they are but checks which often render the next outbreak more alarming. The force of punishment will be found to resemble the application of power in changing the growth of the tree: weeks, years of confinement, will not effect a complete reformation in the offender. His life may seem to be changed, his habits reformed; but, as he goes out to mingle again with the world, as one occasion after another presents itself to him, his former passions begin to revive, those early impressions take possession of him, and he becomes the same that he was originally, only that his degraded position renders him far less able to resist the temptation to do wrong. Impressions and habits acquired in youth are proverbially lasting. With characteristic eloquence and fervor has Lord Brougham illustrated the peculiar importance of early training. In a Speech delivered in the House of Lords in 1835 upon one of those measures which have conferred so much glory on his name as well as benefit upon his countrymen, he said, "If at a very early age a system of instruction is pursued by which a certain degree of independent feeling is created in the child's mind, while all mutinous and perverse disposition is avoided, — if this system be followed up by a constant instruction in the principles of virtue, and a corresponding advancement in intellectual pursuits, — if, during the most critical years of his life, his understanding and his feelings are accustomed only to sound principles and pure and innocent impressions, it will become almost impossible that he should afterward take to vicious courses, because these will be utterly alien to the whole nature of his being. It will be as difficult for him to become criminal, because as foreign to his confirmed habits, as it would be for one of your lordships to go out and rob on the highway. Thus, to commence the education of youth at the tender age on which I have laid so much stress, will, I feel confident, be the same means of guarding society against crimes. I trust every thing to habit, — habit, upon which, in all ages, the lawgiver, as well as the schoolmaster, has mainly placed his reliance, — habit, which makes every thing easy, and casts all difficulties upon the deviation from the wonted course. Make sobriety a habit, and intemperance will be hateful and hard; make prudence a habit, and reckless profligacy will be as contrary to the nature of the child, grown an adult, as the most atrocious crimes are to any of your lordships. Give a child the habit of sacredly regarding truth, of carefully respecting the property of others, of scrupulously abstaining from all acts of improvidence which can involve him in distress, and he will just as little think of lying or cheating or stealing, or running in debt, as of rushing into an element in which he cannot breathe."

The thought may strike some, however, that children can receive moral discipline at home; that parents are best enabled to understand the disposition of their children, and can consequently apply the requisite training with more success than any one else; and, most of all, because it is their especial duty so to do. So we might say, with almost as much reason, that parents could teach their children the elementary branches of knowledge; in the first place, because it is in their province to know the peculiar turn of mind possessed by their children, and also for the equally plausible reason, that they are under a great obligation to educate them. Now, there is much truth in the observation of Seneca's, that people carry their neighbors' faults in a bag before them, which are easily to be seen, and their own behind them unseen; and, without doing parents too much injustice, we may say that they are inclined to carry the failings of their children tied up with their own. The fact is, generally speaking, parents are so confident that their children do not lack in honesty and integrity, at a time when these principles should be forcibly impressed upon them, that they let the occasion for moral training pass until bad habits are deeply rooted in their character. There are, we know, many cheering exceptions; yet, if moral instruction is neglected in the school, to a majority of the scholars that neglect will nowhere be provided for, until some bad results have ensued.

To carry out, then, the primal purpose of our system of education, instructors should seek to mould the character of their pupils. Supervisors and committee-men should require a faithful discharge of this trust. When they come to examine the school, if the standard of intellectual attainments is not so high as might be desirable, they should yet bear testimony to its advancement, if they find that those "virtues which adorn life" have been held up in all their attractiveness to the imitation of the pupil.

Thus have we seen that the system itself contemplates the culture of the heart as well as the mind; and that it is wise, practical, and just in doing so. We now propose to show that this object is generally disregarded, if not entirely lost sight of, in our common schools; and to illustrate, if possible, the means

5

whereby it can be more completely carried into operation. In the first place, the present state of society testifies to a neglect somewhere of inculcating habits of rectitude. There is a want of CONSCIENCE in the community. The prevalence of crime, as seen by the returns of public prosecutors and magistrates, is but a small part of the evidence of this fact. We might as well judge of a man's wealth by his dress, as to form an opinion on public morals by the number of punishable offences committed. And, indeed, the records of courts furnish but incomplete evidence of the number of punishable offences actually committed; for where one criminal is brought to the bar of justice, ten escape detection. We have the authority of a very eminent Judge for this remark. But there are wrongs which are not punishable by the law, being too small and undefinable for its cognizance. It is the bad faith which enters into contracts, and deceives the honest purchaser, or dupes the confiding vendor; the baseness which conspires to wink down credit; the avarice which greedily takes advantage of poverty, or the craft which converts it into a weapon of fraud; the scandal which sets neighbor against neighbor; the fretful harshness which clouds the domestic fireside; the ingratitude which spurns parental influence; the selfishness which would trade in principles, and bargain away public measures for private gain, — these, and such as these, are the conclusive proofs of public vice. Even the deplorable appearances which penury exhibits are counterfeited, and we hesitate to give alms lest we should encourage an impostor. The benevolent man distrusts the beggar who asks for a night's lodging, and turns him away, fearful that he might prove an assassin or a robber; or he reluctantly calls him back, lest he should revenge himself by burning his barn. There are common symptoms which show a patient's sickness, though they do not indicate the particular nature of his disease. So this mutual distrust, which characterizes the dealings of men, indicates the debility of public morals, and points with unerring certainty to the neglect of early discipline.

But an inspection of the schools will afford us the most reliable evidence on this subject. From the system of instruction now pursued in our best common schools, a scholar of ordinary capacity is enabled to become a good reader, writer, and speller; to acquire a very good knowledge of geography and arithmetic, and a little insight into natural philosophy, physiology, grammar, and history, as well as to gain some habits of order and correct deportment. It is true also that in some schools considerable efforts are bestowed on moral culture: this, however, depends upon the peculiar character of the teacher. Yet it cannot be denied, that intellectual improvement is treated as of paramount importance; and that, if any attempts are made at moral training, they are purely incidental; being considered collateral to the other lessons. Surely no one will think of reproaching teachers for this condition of things; for they are governed by the public opinion of the district or town they teach in, as much as the statesman is governed by the public opinion of the country. The voice of the district is silent on the subject. The committee who examined or engaged them did not allude to that part of their duty, or inquire into their qualifications for discharging it. If the teacher goes through the term in harmony, and succeeds in advancing his pupils in an ordinary degree in the common branches, he is acknowledged to have accomplished his entire duty.

In attempting to show the manner in which the right development of character may be blended with the development of the mental faculties, it might be proper to advert to the method a teacher could pursue with the greatest success. A very imperfect idea only of any policy can be given, inasmuch as the duty must be left to his own discretion. No set plan can be adhered to; neither could text-books be used to advantage. He should not have an appointed time for such an exercise, nor resort to formal lectures, nor rely upon the studied maxims which moralists have framed in the closet, nor depend upon the stereotyped precepts of philosophers. As the sentiments he inculcates are addressed to the heart, so also from the heart should they spring. Every one knows that the events which transpire in and about the school-room furnish too frequent opportunities for this species of instruction. These acts of turpitude he should heed, and make the subject of his lessons. Report comes to him that some of his pupils have been guilty of insulting and ridiculing an aged and infirm person. He might give them time to reflect upon the nature of their act, and to decide themselves whether it was right or wrong. Then let him show the claims which age, combined with feebleness, has upon our respect and sympathy, and expose the cruelty and shame of that conduct which would increase its misfortunes. He learns, perhaps, that a pupil has used profane language during an intermission. As he requires the school to pause, let him speak in simple language of the omnipotence and omnipresence of the Creator; of the commandment which he has ordained, that none should take his name in vain. By referring to some of the faculties, mental and physical, with which he has been endowed, let the teacher call forth the gratitude, not only of that pupil but the whole school, for the wonderful goodness of their Maker. By reminding them of his compassion and tenderness, his infinite wisdom and power, let him inspire them with love and reverence for his name. Envy and jealousy he will see prominent in the character of his fairest pupils: let him show that the heart was not made for such feelings; that, if they are nurtured there, no room will be found for noble and generous sentiments. Quarrels will occur in which blows will be dealt lustily: a few simple illustrations will prove that force is a dangerous and imperfect arbiter of justice. If unhappily falsehood prevails, let him make haste to supplant a habit, so fearful and pernicious, though every thing else be laid aside. Let him show the great inconvenience a man must experience in whose word no confidence can be reposed. The fable of the shepherd-boy who gave false alarms to the distant workmen of the approach of wolves, so that when the wolves really came his cries were in vain, will show that lying is unprofitable in the end. But his chief object should be to exhibit the moral turpitude of the habit, — the facility with which it leads to deeper guilt, — the manifold evils which it engenders in the community; and thus to impress upon the minds of his pupils a sacred regard for truth. Such, it might seem, would be the course which a high-minded and zealous teacher would pursue in imparting moral instruction. But, whatever be his method, it is quite certain that a successful performance of his duty in this respect implies great capacity. Extensive learning will not be a sufficient qualification. An accurate and comprehensive knowledge of the sciences may have given vigor to his mind; he may be familiar with the classic pages of Thucydides and Homer, Horace and Livy; he may be versed in the philosophy of history, and yet lack in the essential elements of his art. He must possess native talent, a clear insight of human character, agreeable address, extemporaneous powers of speech. He must be a clear-thinking, conscientious, practical man; and it will be impossible for him to fail in his undertaking. Such a teacher will win the respect and esteem of his pupils: they will imitate his example, and cherish his counsel.

Now, the inquiry will naturally be made if the teachers of common schools have these qualifications. There are some who are thus qualified. They are those who in other professions would rise to eminence by the zeal and ability with which they now advance our youth in intellectual culture. But they are an exception to the common standard. The majority of teachers, however, are quite young. They are preparing themselves for other duties, which they consider more important to their own interests, if not the interests of the public. Not experienced sufficiently in their art to excel in its ordinary labors, they do not stand far enough above their pupils to succeed in this higher and more difficult branch of instruction.

Before, then, moral education can be successfully promoted, the right kind of teachers must be employed. There is but one way of obtaining them, and that is by paying them liberal salaries. All are not philanthropists. Here and there, it is true, may be found persons disinterested enough to devote their energies to the public good, for their daily bread alone. But it is the height of absurdity to expect that men of talent and learning will continue in so arduous an occupation as that of teaching for small compensation, when in less laborious pursuits they can acquire opulence. The average pay received by male teachers throughout the Commonwealth, as appears from the last annual report of the learned Secretary of the Board of Education, is $37.26 per month. The average length of schools being seven months and a half, the yearly salary of the teacher would therefore be $279.45; out of which he must pay for his board and all other expenses. Hardly adequate to support one man respectably, it entirely excludes the circumstance of his having a family, implying a self-denial of the common uses of social life. The natural presumption is, that a teacher is not exempt from the calamities that sometimes befall men; that he buys a few books and a little stationary; that he is as unwilling as any one to wear ragged clothes; and, uncertain of continued employment in one place, that he incurs some expense in changing his locality. But the standard price which he receives ignores any such presumption. In regard to the payment of female teachers, we might suppose that a different rule would prevail; that in a community where woman holds a high moral, social, and intellectual position, — where marked deference is paid to her character, — where the great superiority of her influence as a parent and a teacher is acknowledged, — one might indeed suppose that she would be liberally rewarded for her services, especially when those services are rendered in her peculiar sphere of duty, — that of teaching. Strange as it may appear, such is not the case; while her labor, apparently not so responsible, is often more wearing than the labor of the schoolmaster. It seems that the average pay of female teachers is $15.36 per month. When it is remembered that all the expenses of living are to be deducted from the amount paid at this rate, her real income shrinks into the merest trifle. There is not an occupation in which intelligent young women can be employed that does not present greater pecuniary inducements. Under such circumstances it must be a matter of surprise that we have as good teachers, both male and female, as now have charge of our schools. Will any one, then, for a moment suppose that persons of greater ability than they will be induced to engage or continue in such an employment, when wealth and influence and happiness point in another direction? Laying aside suppositions, let us see what the facts are. With the majority of those now engaged in the business, teaching is a temporary employment. Some are teaching during their college vacations, intending, as soon as they graduate, to commence their professional studies; — they are perhaps our future judges, or clergymen, or sagacious merchants; others are already abandoning the business to enter upon mercantile pursuits. As soon as they have acquired experience, so that their services are truly valuable to the public, they find that their future prospects are to be sacrificed if they continue longer in the profession. Thus, instead of retaining persons in this most important of all professions, we drive them out of it to adorn and exalt other occupations. Many of the ablest men in each of our learned professions were once school-teachers: if a proper reward had encouraged them to remain in that capacity, how visible at this day would be the influence which they would have exerted upon their pupils! It is clear, then, that the only means by which we can retain teachers who have the requisite talent and ability, is by paying them adequate salaries. Then our schools can furnish moral as well as intellectual instruction; and the object which our system of education contemplates can in a great degree be accomplished.

Fully aware that the people are peculiarly sensitive on the subject of taxation, especially when no tangible results are to follow its increase, we do not hesitate to say that the interests of education demand a far greater expenditure of money. The spirit which has characterized the people of the Commonwealth, in their past efforts to advance the cause, promises favorable action on the subject. In an age when astonishing improvements in every art and every science are being developed, — when nature, in her most regal and opposing state, bends to the energy of man, — when countless sums are lavished to gratify and satiate every sense, how mortifying and discreditable that a great moral cause should languish! Even if the contribution which would be required for this purpose could in any way be felt by the poorest citizen, it could not be felt as a burden; for he might regard it as an investment the most profitable and secure, — the income of which would return to his own door full of blessings upon his declining days. When solicited to double the tax which he had formerly paid for school-purposes, regarding his own interest merely, and not that of the public, he might sincerely say, "Yes, out of my limited means I am content to pay freely for such an object. By paying the teacher more, am I not increasing his usefulness? Am I not doing something to bring up my children in knowledge and integrity? Will they not be a greater comfort to me, and more happy and prosperous themselves? Besides, in a few years, much mischief in the community may be diminished, and there will be a smaller tax on me and mine to support criminals and prisons. If all are taught to do their duty as citizens, I shall not suffer for their neglect of doing so." Though the correctness of his reasoning will be admitted, the argument in this behalf should be placed on higher grounds than individual prosperity. The benefits to be derived by the public as exhibited in the abatement of many social evils, — in the diffusion of rational happiness, — in the gains of honest industry, such should be the inducements to this worthy undertaking.

In conclusion, we submit that for reasons too apparent to be alluded to, and too urgent to be disregarded, more attention should be devoted to the true aim and purpose of education, — to a more complete operation of the system. More than the past has needed, will the future require the benefits which it unfolds. Let the teacher's vocation be elevated, and advantages will accrue to the State, compared with which, exuberant harvests, a thriving commerce, and an overflowing treasury, will be but small resources. We should form a wise and generous precedent in this matter, below which indifference will not suffer us to fall. We should engage in the enterprise with a determination to carry it forward to the highest degree of success. It may be "absurd to expect, but it is not absurd to pursue, perfection."

www.ingramcontent.com/pod-product-compliance
Lightning Source LLC
LaVergne TN
LVHW011136110826
845150LV00008B/2369

9781418193713